ART
OF THE 20TH CENTURY

2000 TASCHEN DIARY
www.taschen.com

Art of the 20th Century

The art of the twentieth century, like the parallel advances in science and technology, undoubtedly comprises the most inventive and progressive era in the entire history of art. The styles, movements and schools of art seem innumerable. Again and again, artists not only discussed, questioned and rejected former definitions of the term "art" in theory, but extended and redefined it through their work and innovations. However, the field has again narrowed, artists have come closer to each other in their approach and art has become more international.

Just as the Impressionists were held in derision by the public at the end of the 19th century but are now the widely admired stars of museums and exhibitions, artists such as Picasso and Braque, Matisse or Derain, Kirchner and Beckmann, Kandinsky or Klee, Mondrian and Malevich, Chagall or Dalí, Pollock and Rothko, Warhol or Lichtenstein, Polke and Richter, were first considered avant-garde and had to fight long and hard for their success. Today, they already rank as classic modern artists – just as the styles they represent, such as Fauvism and Expressionism, Cubism or Abstraction, Surrealism and Pop Art, Action Painting or Photorealism, are known to every lover of art. This diary presents a few masterpieces from the rich store of 20th-century art.

Die Kunst des 20. Jahrhunderts ist – vergleichbar mit den Neuerungen in Wissenschaft und Technik – wohl die an Fortschritten reichste Epoche der Kunstgeschichte. Unübersehbar scheint die Zahl der Stile, Strömungen und Schulen. Immer wieder haben die Künstler nicht nur in der Theorie den Begriff „Kunst" diskutiert, in Frage gestellt und verworfen, sondern durch ihre Arbeit und ihre „Erfindungen" auch neu definiert und ausprobiert. Doch die Grenzen sind enger geworden, die Künstler einander nähergerückt, die Kunst ist internationaler geworden.

So wie die Impressionisten – am Ende des 19. Jahrhunderts vom Publikum noch verspottet – heute die vielbewunderten „Stars" der Museen und Ausstellungen sind, so zählten auch Künstler wie Picasso und Braque, Matisse oder Derain, Kirchner und Beckmann, Kandinsky oder Klee, Mondrian und Malewitsch, Chagall oder Dalí, Pollock und Rothko, Warhol oder Lichtenstein, Polke und Richter in ihren Anfängen zur „Avantgarde" und mußten lange für ihren Erfolg kämpfen. Doch auch sie gehören bereits heute zu den Klassikern der Moderne – so wie die von ihnen vertretenen Stile, wie Fauvismus und Expressionismus, Kubismus oder Abstraktion, Surrealismus und Pop Art, Action Painting oder Fotorealismus jedem Kunstliebhaber vertraut sind. Das Diary stellt einige Meisterwerke aus dem reichen Schatz der Kunst des 20. Jahrhunderts vor.

Martin Kippenberger
Good idea today – done tomorrow
1983. Oil on canvas, 160 x 133 cm
Private collection

Art of the 20th Century

Le XXᵉ siècle – et cela vaut aussi pour la science et les technologies – est sans doute l'époque de l'histoire de l'art la plus fertile en évolutions. Dénombrer tous les styles, les courants et les écoles qu'il a vu naître est une tâche difficile. Les artistes n'ont pas cessé de discuter, de remettre en question, de rejeter le concept d'« art », et ce pas seulement sur le plan théorique. Par leur travail et leurs « inventions » ils l'ont aussi redéfini et expérimenté. Mais les frontières se sont rétrécies, les artistes se sont rapprochés et l'art est devenu international.

Les impressionnistes, encore la cible des railleries à la fin du XIXᵉ siècle, sont aujourd'hui les « stars » inégalées des musées et des expositions. Et si des artistes comme Picasso et Braque, Matisse, Derain, Kirchner et Beckmann, Kandinsky, Klee, Mondrian et Malevitch, Chagall, Dalí, Pollock, Rothko, Warhol, Lichtenstein, Polke et Richter faisaient encore à leurs débuts partie de l'avant-garde et durent longtemps se battre pour être reconnus et appréciés, ils sont, eux aussi, déjà considérés comme des classiques des temps modernes. Les styles qu'ils représentent, comme le fauvisme, l'expressionnisme, le cubisme, l'abstraction, le surréalisme, le pop art, l'action painting et le réalisme photographique sont aujourd'hui bien connus des amateurs d'art. Le présent agenda offre quelques chefs-d'œuvre choisis dans le trésor artistique du XXᵉ siècle.

Vergelijkbaar met de vernieuwingen die zich voordeden in de wetenschap en techniek is de 20e eeuw ook voor de kunst de vooruitstrevendste eeuw in de kunstgeschiedenis. Deze eeuw telt ongelooflijk veel stijlen, stromingen en scholen. Nog nooit eerder hebben kunstenaars zo veel over het begrip 'kunst' gediscussieerd; zij hebben in theorie én praktijk vragen gesteld en antwoorden gezocht, en door hun werk en 'ervaringen' ontwikkelden zij nieuwe ideeën. Daardoor zijn grenzen vervaagd, kunstenaars zijn elkaar nader gekomen en de kunst is internationaler geworden.

Zo is het ook met de impressionisten gegaan; aan het einde van de 19e eeuw werden zij nog door het grote publiek uitgelachen, maar tegenwoordig zijn zij door musea en tentoonstellingen als veel bewonderde 'sterren' binnengehaald. Ook schilders als Picasso en Braque, Matisse en Derain, Kirchner en Beckmann, Kandinsky en Klee, Mondriaan en Malevitsj, Chagall en Dalí, Pollock en Rothko, Warhol en Lichtenstein, Polke en Richter behoorden in eerste instantie tot de 'voorhoede'. Zij moesten lang wachten op erkenning. Tegenwoordig worden zij echter gerekend tot de eerste moderne kunstenaars en vertegenwoordigen zij de stijlen die elke kunstliefhebber kent, zoals Fauvisme en Expressionisme, maar ook abstracte kunst en Surrealisme, Pop Art en de 'nieuwe wilden'. In deze agenda vindt u een collectie meesterwerken uit de rijke schatkamer van de 20e-eeuwse kunst.

Piet Mondrian
Composition No. II. Composition with Blue and Red
1929. Oil on canvas, 40.3 x 32.1 cm
New York, The Museum of Modern Art / © Mondrian / Holtzman Trust, c/o Beeldrecht, Amsterdam, Holland / VG Bild-Kunst, Bonn 1999

Pablo Picasso
Les Demoiselles d'Avignon
1907. Oil on canvas, 243.9 x 233.7 cm
New York, The Museum of Modern Art / © Succession Picasso / VG Bild-Kunst, Bonn 1999

Wassily Kandinsky
Two Ovals (Composition No. 218)
1919. Oil on canvas, 107 x 89.5 cm
St. Petersburg, Russian State Museum / © VG Bild-Kunst, Bonn 1999

Max Ernst
The Tottering Woman
1923. Oil on canvas, 130.5 x 97.5 cm
Düsseldorf, Kunstsammlung Nordrhein-Westfalen / © VG Bild-Kunst, Bonn 1999

Kasimir Malevich
Suprematism
c. 1917. Oil on canvas, 80 x 80 cm
Krasnodar, Lunatscharski-Museum

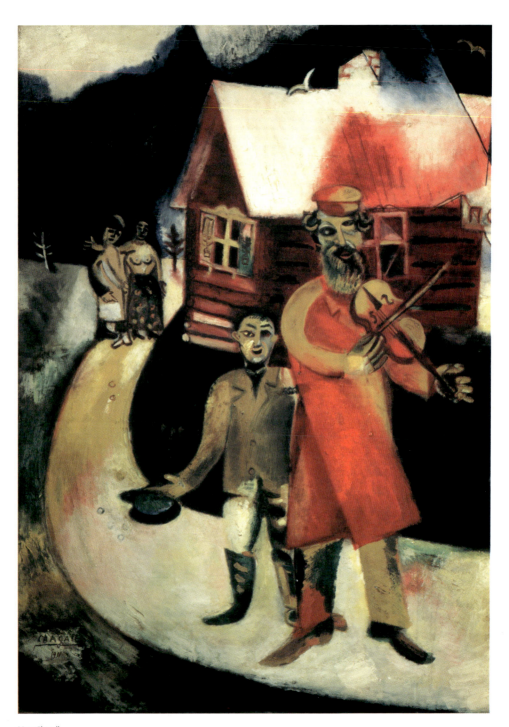

Marc Chagall
The Violinist
1911–1914. Oil on canvas, 94.5 x 69.5 cm
Düsseldorf, Kunstsammlung Nordrhein-Westfalen / © VG Bild-Kunst, Bonn 1999

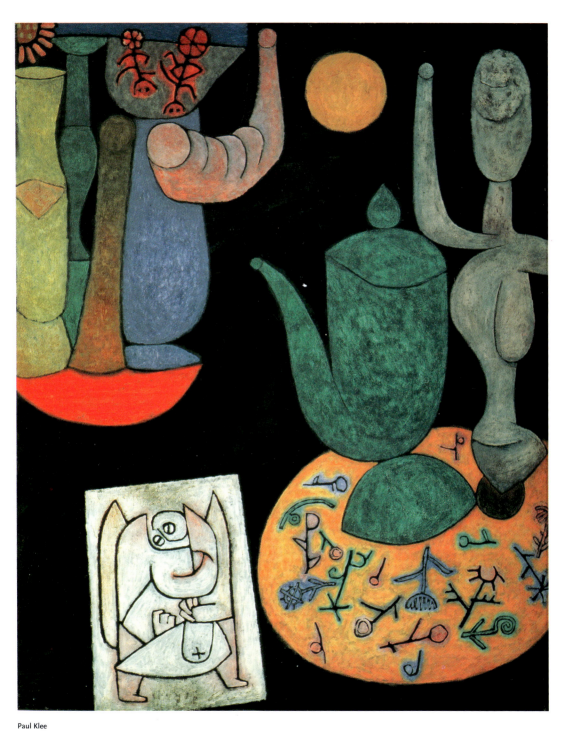

Paul Klee
Untitled
1940 [001]. Oil on canvas on a stretcher, 100 x 80.5 cm
Switzerland, private collection / © *VG Bild-Kunst, Bonn 1999*

Cy Twombly
Untitled (Roma)
1962. Oil, crayon and pencil on canvas, 199 x 240.5 cm
Private collection / © 1999 Cy Twombly

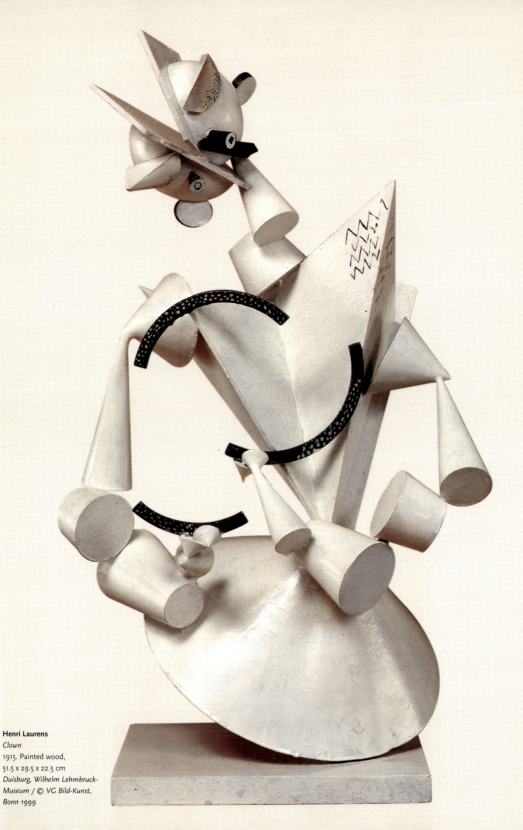

Henri Laurens
Clown
1915. Painted wood,
51.5 x 29.5 x 22.5 cm
Duisburg, Wilhelm Lehmbruck-
Museum / © VG Bild-Kunst,
Bonn 1999

Francis Bacon
Study for Self-Portrait (triptych, central panel)
1985/86. Oil on canvas, 198 x 147.5 cm
London, Marlborough International Fine Art / © VG Bild-Kunst, Bonn 1999

Willem de Kooning
Woman I
1950–1952. Oil on canvas, 192.7 x 147.3 cm
New York, The Museum of Modern Art / © Willem de Kooning Revocable Trust / VG Bild-Kunst, Bonn 1999

Jeff Koons
Pink Panther
1988. Porcelain, 104.1 x 52.1 x 48.3 cm
Private collection / © 1999 Jeff Koons

Victor Vasarely
Vega 200
1968. Acrylic on canvas, 200 x 200 cm
Private collection / © VG Bild-Kunst, Bonn 1999

Ernst Ludwig Kirchner
The Red Tower in Halle
1915. Oil on canvas, 120 x 90.5 cm
Essen, Museum Folkwang / © 1999 Dr. Wolfgang & Ingeborg Henze-Ketterer, Wichtrach / Bern

Max Beckmann
Self-Portrait with Red Scarf
1917. Oil on canvas, 80 x 60 cm
Stuttgart, Staatsgalerie Stuttgart / © VG Bild-Kunst, Bonn 1999

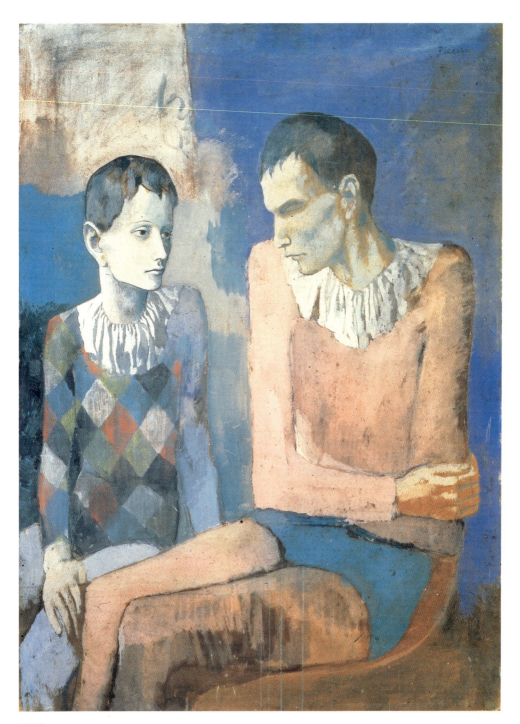

Pablo Picasso
Acrobat and Young Harlequin
1905. Gouache on cardboard, 105 x 76 cm
Private collection / © Succession Picasso / VG Bild-Kunst, Bonn 1999

PARADE AMOUREUSE

Francis Picabia

Love Parade

1917. Oil on cardboard, 96.5 x 73.7 cm

Chicago (IL), Morton G. Neumann Collection / © VG Bild-Kunst, Bonn 1999

Duane Hanson
Supermarket Lady
1969. Painted fibreglass, polyester and clothing, shopping cart with product packs. Figure: c. 166 x 70 x 70 cm
Aachen, Ludwig Forum für Internationale Kunst / © Wesla Hanson, Davie (FL)

August Macke
Hat Shop
1914. Oil on canvas, 60.5 x 50.5 cm
Essen, Museum Folkwang

Joan Miró
Ladders Cross the Blue Sky in a Wheel of Fire
1953. Oil on canvas, 116 x 89 cm
Private collection / © VG Bild-Kunst, Bonn 1999

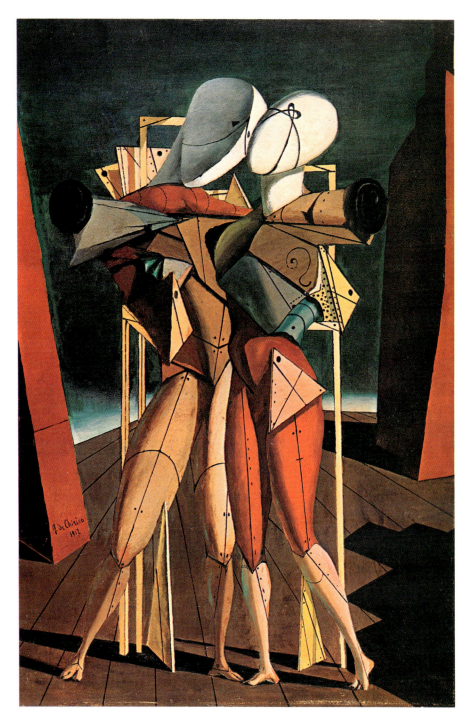

Giorgio de Chirico
Hector and Andromache
1917. Oil on canvas, 90 x 60 cm
Milan, private collection / © VG Bild-Kunst, Bonn 1999

Jackson Pollock
Number 4
1950. Oil, enamel paint and aluminum paint on canvas, 124.1 x 94.3 cm
Pittsburgh (PA), Carnegie Museum of Art, Gift of Frank S. Kaplan / © VG Bild-Kunst, Bonn 1999

Yves Klein
Blue Sponge Relief (RE 19)
1958. Pigment in synthetic resin on sponges, gravel, and composition board, 200 x 165 cm
Cologne, Museum Ludwig, Ludwig Donation / © VG Bild-Kunst, Bonn 1999

Roy Lichtenstein
M-Maybe (A Girl's Picture)
1965. Magna on canvas, 152 x 152 cm
Cologne, Museum Ludwig, Ludwig Donation / © VG Bild-Kunst, Bonn 1999

Georges Braque
Fruit Bowl and Glass
1912. Charcoal and papiers collés, 62 x 44.5 cm
Private collection / © VG Bild-Kunst, 1999

Sigmar Polke
Lovers II
1965. Oil and lacquer on canvas, 200 x 140 cm
Private collection / © 1999 Sigmar Polke / Galerie Klein, Bad Münstereifel

René Magritte
The Empire of Light
1954. Oil on canvas, 146 x 113.7 cm
Brussels, Musées Royaux des Beaux-Arts / © VG Bild-Kunst, Bonn 1999

Egon Schiele
Seated Woman with Bent Knee
1917. Gouache, watercolour and black crayon, 46 x 30.5 cm
Prague, Národni Galeri

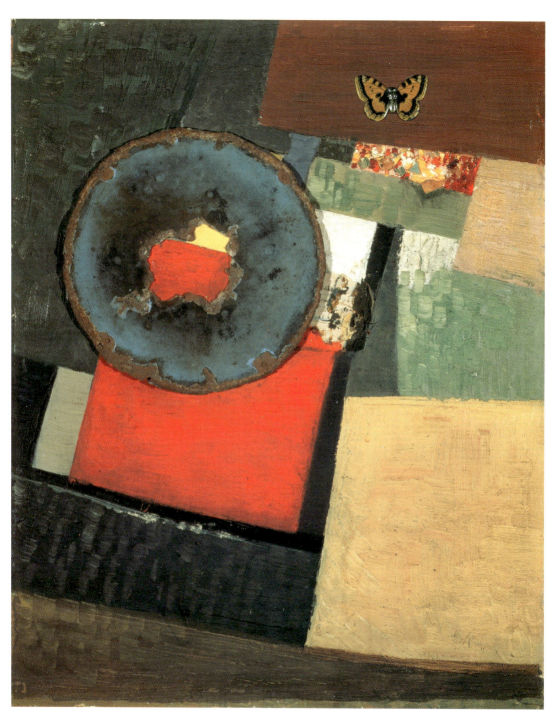

Kurt Schwitters
Maraak, Variation I
1930. Oil and assemblage on cardboard, 46 x 37 cm
Venice, Peggy Guggenheim Collection / © VG Bild-Kunst, Bonn 1999

Gustav Klimt
Danae
c. 1907/08. Oil on canvas, 77 x 83 cm
Private collection

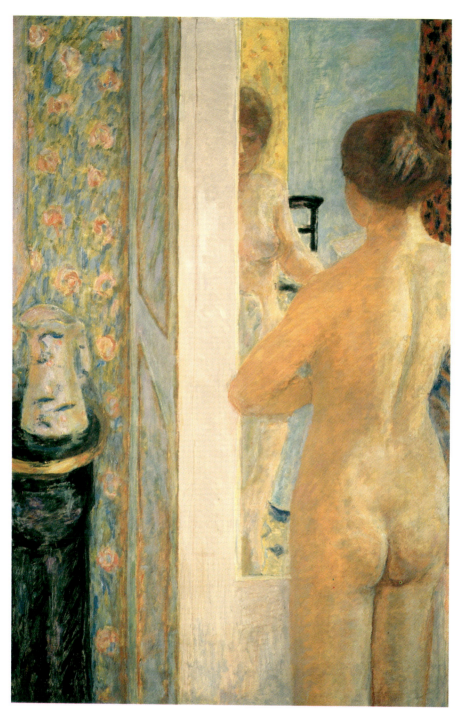

Pierre Bonnard
The Toilette
c. 1908. Oil on canvas, 119 x 79 cm
Paris, Musée d'Orsay / © VG Bild-Kunst, Bonn 1999

Salvador Dalí

Leda Atomica

1949. Oil on canvas, 61.1 x 45.3 cm

Figueras, Fundación Gala-Salvador Dalí / © Salvador Dalí: Demart Pro Arte BV 1999

Sam Francis
Round the World
1958/59. Oil on canvas, 274.3 x 321.3 cm
Private collection / © VG Bild-Kunst, Bonn 1999

Previous page:
Christo & Jeanne-Claude
Surrounded Islands
1980–1983. Fabric, 603 850 m²
Biscayne Bay Greater Miami (FL) / © Christo 1980–1983

Henri Matisse
Spanish Woman with Tambourine
1909. Oil on canvas, 92 x 73 cm
Moscow, Pushkin Museum, S. I. Shchukin Collection / © Succession H. Matisse / VG Bild-Kunst, Bonn 1999

Philip Taaffe
Bad Seed
1996. Mixed media on canvas, 262 x 282 cm
Private collection / © 1999 Philip Taaffe, New York

Frida Kahlo
Self-Portrait with Monkey
1938. Oil on hardboard, 40.6 x 30.5 cm
Buffalo (NY), Albright-Knox Art Gallery, Bequest of A. Conger Goodyear / © 1999 Instituto Nacional de Bellas Artes, Mexico

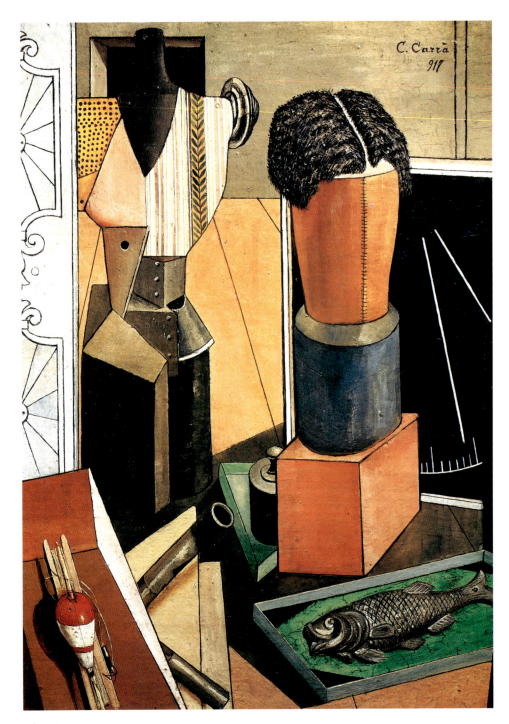

Carlo Carrà

The Enchanted Room

1917. Oil on canvas, 65 x 52 cm

Milan, private collection / © VG Bild-Kunst, Bonn 1999

Richard Lindner
Meeting
1953. Oil on canvas, 152.4 x 182.9 cm
New York, The Museum of Modern Art / © VG Bild-Kunst, Bonn 1999

Mark Rothko
Untitled
1957. Oil on canvas, 143 x 138 cm
Private collection / © Kate Rothko-Prizel & Christopher Rothko / VG Bild-Kunst, Bonn 1999

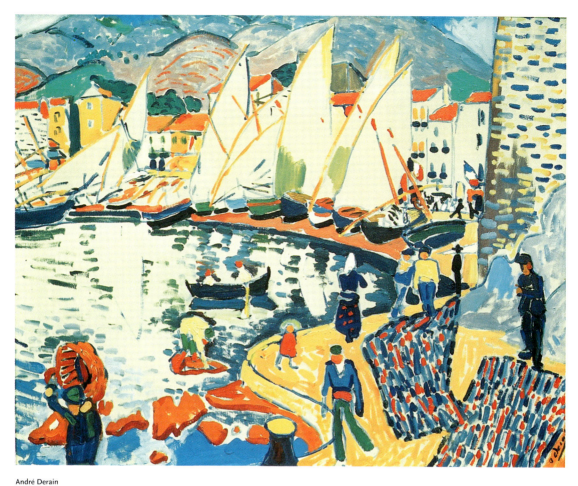

André Derain
Drying Sails
1905. Oil on canvas, 82 x 101 cm
Moscow, Pushkin Museum, I. A. Morosov Collection / © VG Bild-Kunst, Bonn 1999

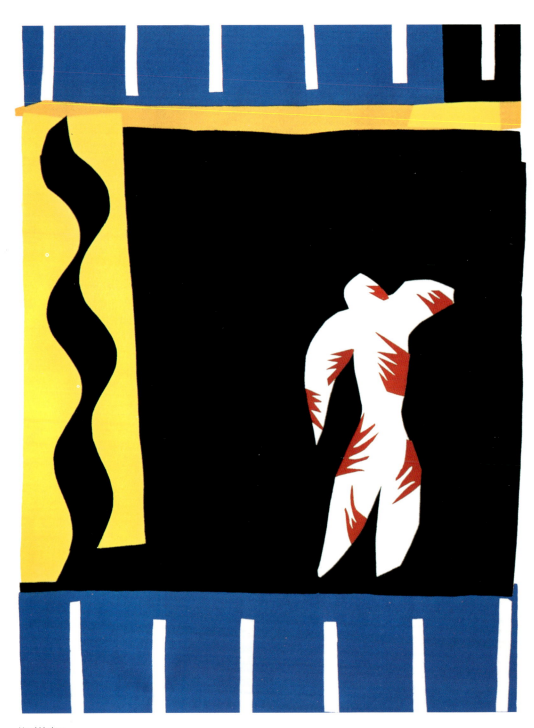

Henri Matisse
The Clown ("Jazz")
1943. Stencil
© *Succession H. Matisse / VG Bild-Kunst, Bonn 1999*

Gerhard Richter
S. D. I.
1986. Oil on canvas, two parts, 320 x 400 cm
Napa (CA), Hess Collection / © Gerhard Richter, Cologne

Alexej von Jawlensky
Girl with Peonies
1909. Oil on cardboard, mounted on plywood, 101 x 75 cm
Wuppertal, Von der Heydt-Museum / © VG Bild-Kunst, Bonn 1999

Albert Oehlen
Untitled
1993. Oil on fabric (imprinted), 240 x 240 cm. WVZ No.4/93
Private collection

Franz Marc
Deer in the Woods II
1914. Oil on canvas, 110 x 100.5 cm
Karlsruhe, Staatliche Kunsthalle

Tom Wesselmann
Great American Nude No. 98
1967. Five canvases arranged behind one another in three planes, 250 x 380 x 130 cm
Cologne, Museum Ludwig / © VG Bild-Kunst, Bonn 1999

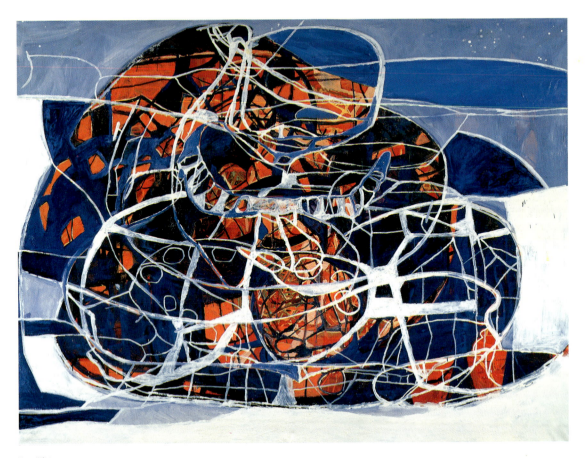

Terry Winters
Phase Plane Portrait
1994. Oil and alkyd resin on linen, 274.3 x 365.8 cm
Private collection

Edward Hopper
"Chop Suey"
1929. Oil on canvas, 81.3 x 96.5 cm
Private collection

George Grosz
Republican Automatons
1920. Watercolour, ink and India ink on cardboard, 60 x 47.3 cm
New York, The Metropolitan Museum of Art / © VG Bild-Kunst, Bonn 1999

Fernand Léger
The Stairway
1914. Oil on canvas, 130 x 100 cm
New York, The Museum of Modern Art / © VG Bild-Kunst, Bonn 1999

Lyonel Feininger
Gelmeroda IX
1926. Oil on canvas, 108 x 80 cm
Essen, Museum Folkwang / © VG Bild-Kunst, Bonn 1999

riedensreich Hundertwasser

936 *Das 30 Tage Fax Bild |* 936 *The 30 Day Fax Picture*

ienna 1994. Mixed media, 151 x 130 cm

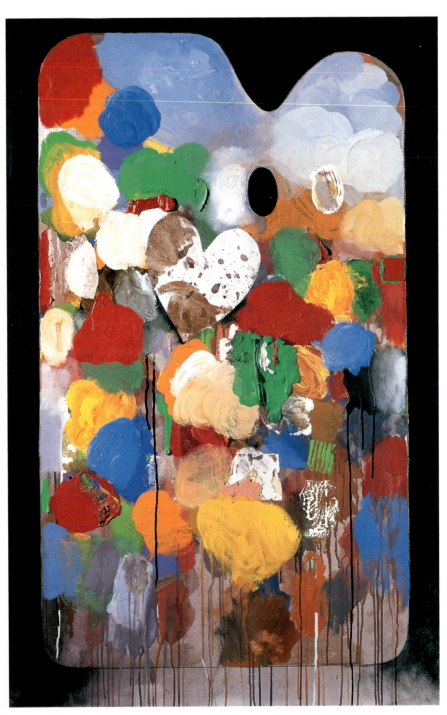

Jim Dine
Pleasure Palette
1969. Oil, glass, paper on canvas, 152 x 102 cm
Cologne, Museum Ludwig, Ludwig Donation

Yves Tanguy
The Five Strangers
1941. Oil on canvas, 98.1 x 81.3 cm
Hartford (CT), Wadsworth Atheneum, The Ella Galup Sumner Collection / © VG Bild-Kunst, Bonn 1999

Otto Dix
Metropolis (triptych, central panel)
1927/28. Mixed media on wood, 181 x 200 cm
Stuttgart, Galerie der Stadt Stuttgart / © VG Bild-Kunst, Bonn 1999